gama®

Învăț să citesc!®

Rățușca cea urâtă

Ugly Duckling

după H. C. Andersen

One beautiful summer, a mother duck sat patiently[1] on her five eggs.

*Caută cuvintele în dicționarul de pe ultima pagină

One day the ducklings[2] hatched[3]: four were white and one was... *gray!*

The duck and the other ducklings were surprised to see he was different.

When the other ducks saw him, they laughed and called him "the ugly duckling".

Even his brothers were teasing[4] him all the time and nobody wanted to play with him. The ugly duckling was very sad and lonely.

Mother duck took him under her wing[5], but she soon[6] realized he can't be her baby: a duckling quacks[7], but the ugly duckling didn't.

One day, poor duckling left[8] his home and went to live with an old woman. The lady also had a cat and a hen[9]. The cat played and purred[10] and the hen laid eggs[11]. But the ugly duckling couldn't do either[12] and felt useless.

From the old woman's backyard[13], the duckling went to a peasant's[14] house, but got scared of the man's kids and fled[15].

Spring came and the duckling discovered he had grown[16] up and he could now fly!

So he flew right on the lake and landed close to[17] some beautiful swans[18].

The duckling thought they would laugh at him and wanted to leave.

That's when he saw his reflection in the water mirror[19]: once a gray and ugly duckling, he now was a splendid black swan!

Dicţionar

1 patiently – cu răbdare, răbdător
2 duckling – pui de raţă
3 (to) hatch – a ieşi din ou
4 (to) tease – a tachina
5 wing – aripă
6 soon – curând
7 (to) quack – a măcăni
8 (to) leave – a pleca, a părăsi
9 hen – găină
10 (to) purr – a toarce
11 (to) lay eggs – a face ouă
12 either – nici (una, nici alta)
13 backyard – curte
14 peasant – ţăran
15 (to) flee – a fugi de pericol
16 (to) grow up – a creşte, a se maturiza
17 close to – aproape de
18 swan – lebădă
19 water mirror – luciul apei

www.edituragama.ro